THE
TIPPING
POINT

THE
TIPPING POINT
An Argument for Eliminating Gratuities

PETER CALDON

THE TIPPING POINT
AN ARGUMENT FOR ELIMINATING GRATUITIES

iUniverse books may be ordered through booksellers or by contacting:

iUniverse
1663 Liberty Drive
Bloomington, IN 47403
www.iuniverse.com
1-800-Authors (1-800-288-4677)

ISBN: 978-1-5320-4747-3 (sc)
ISBN: 978-1-5320-4746-6 (e)

Library of Congress Control Number: 2018904526

Print information available on the last page.

iUniverse rev. date: 11/05/2019

CONTENTS

PREFACE

No restaurant is safe; no location is best; no dish is a winner; no team is exceptional. It is impossible to avoid the calamities that can occur in food-service operations, from plumbing backups, refrigerator breakdowns, and late deliveries to no-call no-shows and extreme weather conditions. Unless you have an unrelenting commitment, discipline, and drive to create systems and plans of action to reduce the frequency of or eliminate those disasters you can control, you have no chance of survival.

Business, culinary, and professional schools cannot save you. Neither can food channels and social media. Lessons learned from hands-on experience are your only hope. Combining those lessons with education from leading institutions aligned with hospitality can increase the likelihood of success. The speed of change and your response to it are good indicators of how in tune you are with market realities on all sides of the restaurant equation to bring competing interests and resources to bear on the most pressing need at the time to keep moving forward.

Eliminating tipping may be unpopular now as a solution to government overreach to balance wages and benefits to one segment of the industry with an unfortunate unintended consequence to other segments that are otherwise functioning smoothly. I firmly believe in the greater good for all employees in the industry rather than a few. The disruption is understandable, as change brings about uncertainty and anxiety. If it reduces the amount of restaurants available for consumers to choose from; if it increases prices; if it improves the service delivery by professionals who choose service as a career; and if it allows creatives in the kitchens and bars to continue to practice their craft within an inspiring concept, it will be a win in the long run.

We hope you get involved with advocacy groups when the next regulation is proposed that interrupts a special situation for your operation. Chances are it will affect many others as well. To learn is to grow. The lifelong learner will succeed.

ACKNOWLEDGMENTS

Long before the phrase "a student of the game" was uttered by a famous basketball player and athlete to mean love for the sport, preparation, perspiration, and playing through pain, I was a student of hospitality—in particular, the food-service industry—and I continue to be today.

To all the individuals, companies, teachers, and associates who contributed to my growth and development, I bow to you. There are too many to mention, but the list includes my spiritual leader, the Rev. Dr. Clive Neil of the Bedford Central Presbyterian Church in Brooklyn; the Hyatt and Inter-Continental Hotel Corporations that set the foundation for me in the early stages; the Sedixo-Marriots of the world in corporate dining; Great Performances, the premier offsite catering company in New York; and later, the Westchester Country Club. These provided the framework that enabled me to manage, observe, practice, and execute the comparing and contrasting style of leadership and, as an employee, understand how that leadership makes you feel, think, and respond.

To my caring and loving wife, Ann Marie, my thanks for providing the space and time to write undisturbed when I get in the zone—like an open water faucet that cannot be turned off, the mind keeps flowing, and I follow the flow.

Chapter 1

To Tip or Not

To tip or not? At your next dine-out occasion, the decision may depend on the restaurant you choose. Food-service operators are facing enormous challenges, opportunities, and consequences with the choice they make on this critical issue. In New York, there is no better time than now to eliminate tipping in restaurants. New Yorkers will adjust, just as they adjusted to eliminating subway tokens in favor of Metro cards; clacks of foot traffic in retail shopping for clicks in online purchases; and images, icons, emojis and iPhones for everything else.

Ending tipping will not end good service. On the contrary, I will argue that it will elevate service delivery. It gives the team peace of mind so they can focus on customer service because of higher steady income—plus medical insurance, paid leave, and revenue sharing, just like workers in any other retail service industry where the value added by your team is recognized and rewarded.

We are in a bubble of changes in technology, restaurant design, and the broadening definition of hospitality. Why not change tipping too?

We will examine both sides of the coin to help operators make an informed decision, especially those sitting on the fence as they watch what's happening within their competitive set, city, and state. We will take a peep at the impact the choice will have from an operation effectiveness, socioeconomic, and sustainability perspective.

The Fox News website's "Food and Drink" section noted that some familiar names in the restaurant world have come out against tipping:

New York Times restaurant critic Pete Wells has joined a small but growing chorus of those in the food world calling for the abolishment of tips. ... "It is irrational, outdated, ineffective, confusing, prone to abuse and sometimes discriminatory," he wrote in the *New York Times* Dining and Wine section. ... He pointed to well known chefs, such as Tom Colicchio, David Chang, and Daniel Paterson, who admit that tipping should be overhauled, but are unsure how to make up for lost wages or to do it without breaking laws.

Danny Meyers, visionary cofounder of the Union Square Hospitality Group, has been the first to see around the corner to what's coming and make a stand on the uneven distribution of wages in his restaurants. He has rebalanced it to add meaning to the catchphrase "teamwork" for wages.

Operators and owners who keep their ears to the ground with their front-of-the-house staff know or should have knowledge of the range of tips employees make on a daily basis, whether from tip-pooling or not, to create an aggregate of customers' contributions. An analysis of the aggregate can give you an idea of how much more customers would willing to spend on their dining experience if there was no tipping.

When operators consider the size of their payroll budget and add the aggregate of the customer contribution of tips on average, a new wage scale can be determined for all team members. An honest dialogue with your team can bring a fresh perspective and new ideas you've never thought about to the table. What better way to bring the team together than for them to have a say in how they will be paid? What you are really creating is a new team of salespersons in the dining room and bean-counters in the kitchen to reduce waste in food cost and cleaning supplies. A motivation for incentive pay tied to increased revenue targets in the front and cost saving in the back will create a win-win situation for all.

The claim that eliminating tipping and tip credit would lead to lower wages, reduced hours, higher menu prices, and lower customer count is irrational to begin with. At the end of the day, it is merely fearmongering to maintain the status quo.

Yes, higher wages and benefits cut profit margins. Yes, this will lead to an increase in menu prices and possibly lower customer count in the short term. Yes, some restaurants will close, but not because of higher wages, higher menu prices, and lower customer count. Restaurants will close as a result of inefficiencies in design and operating processes and procedures, lack of innovation, poor supervision, ineffective management skills, bad timing, little or no continuous training, and a lack of accountability for standards and productivity.

It is a well-known fact that higher wages lead to greater productivity and lower turnover. Cream always rise to the top.

At the same time as owners worry about eliminating tipping, waiters and bartenders are fighting to keep their tips. Who is fighting for the cooks, dishwashers, and other non-tip employees? After all, they are the ones who do the heavy lifting, cleaning bars and washing the dishes so their coworkers can make big tips.

As an example, New York law specifically permits the sharing of tips by a waiter/server with a busser or similar employee, including bartenders and captains. The Department of Labor (DOL) has included in that definition typical front-of-the-house employees, such as hostesses, short-order cooks, and sushi chefs—employees who "render service" and have contact with the guests—but not chefs, dishwashers, or other nonservice employees who render "no direct service" to the public.

How is it that the dishwasher who scrapes the plates with leftover food when the server is too busy to do so; removes lipstick stains from glasses and cups that customers provide; and painstakingly and patiently sorts through food scraps for the assortment of silverware used to eat the Butter-Poached Lobster with Truffle Potato Ana and Vanilla Hollandaise Brûlée or a Puree of Japanese Artichokes with Early Fall Vegetables and such does not "render service" and offers "no direct service" to the public? It is beyond comprehension.

The time is now to acknowledge the important role food-service employees play in our lives. Paying a living wage is a great start. Let's continue by eliminating disparaging job titles like *busboy*, *dishwasher*, *back-of-the-house*, *front-of-the-house*, and *those who render service*—terms that date back to an ugly, racialized history that originated in aristocratic homes. Alternatively, you could refer to the carefully selected persons on your next flight as *airboys* and *airgirls* or even *tray carriers*. Get it?

To put it differently, using a basketball analogy, the big three of the Miami Heat in 2013 and 2014—Chris Bosh, Dwyane Wade, and LeBron James—could not win back-to-back championships without the help of Ray Allen. When they won, every team member shared in the financial and emotional success. Including all service employees in the tip pool is an incentive and morale booster. Employees not normally sharing in the tip pool will feel more included as part of the team and bring more focus, energy, and cooperation to the overall mission of the restaurant in customer satisfaction.

A good team knows you have to get everybody involved in all the individual tasks necessary to win. The same principle should apply to tipping in food-service operation, or tipping should be eliminated altogether. It has created internal strife between culinary and dining-room employees. It produces two layers of pay, perpetuating an unfair and uneven pay system among and within each variable of gender, race, and task—and by extension, determined class. I believe eliminating tipping will correct the imbalance of wages for all employees in the food-service industry.

To really get to the bottom of this issue, employers and companies should provide statistical evidence to show, by job category for waiters and bartenders and other tip employees, a breakdown by age, ethnicity, and gender. This should be analyzed to see whether it is reflective of the community, city, state, and nation served. Only in this way can it be unquestionably proved that keeping the status quo is not discriminatory.

If that cannot be proved, now is the time to make the change. The DOL must update its guidelines to be in sync with the broadening definition of hospitality under which food service falls. Currently, it is out of touch with the unique reality of today's restaurants.

Tipping encourages servers to upsell customers into ordering more expensive food and wine to boost the size of the check, thereby increasing the size of the tip. This may cause customers with sinister motives to covertly seek more "services" and harass servers—just another issue operators face in making their business a safe place to work, free from harassment both internally and externally.

New York has a long history of convening commissions of enquiry and task forces to collect information on specific issues within industries or communities in response to pressure from advocacy groups seeking changes to improve profits or quality of life. In this instance, two sides—labor unions and advocacy groups— have partnered in supporting the mantra "Fight for Fifteen," seeking to increase the minimum wage to fifteen dollars an hour. This effort started in Chicago and has spread to other major cities, including Seattle and Los Angeles.

The task force on wages in the food-service industry was empaneled by New York Governor Cuomo with a timeline to report back with findings and make recommendations to the governor for resetting the minimum wage. Once the new wages were set to become law, there was significant pushback from certain segments, but the breech in the perimeter for wages in food service was irreparable.

It is a classic example of robbing Peter to pay Paul. Paul, the fast-food guy, was like a virus the Center for Disease Control had never seen before, without any signs of slowing down. In every nook and cranny, Paul was showing up to change the alphabet for kids and some adults too: B for Burger King, M for McDonald's, and W for Wendy's. Diabetes, high blood pressure, and heart disease were spreading in parallel like identical triplets. With businesses putting profit so far ahead of people, and by extension communities, the government came in to make corrections to bring things in balance.

Paul and his friends were making insane profits. These companies paid their executives huge salaries while hiding behind the federal minimum wage law and paying pennies above the minimum wage to everyone else. Is it any wonder Paul and friends are now offering healthy menu choices like salads and grilled meats, just like Peter, and offering higher wages in some instances ahead of the effective date to scale wages to fifteen dollars an hour?

In addition, the government now requires Paul and the rest of the gang with more than fifteen outlets to indicate calorie count on each menu dish and highlight those in which the salt content is higher than the normal daily requirement. Government intervention in restaurant menu preparation to protect customers and by extension communities—thus decreasing the cost of health care—is a result of too long an absence of concern for consumer well-being. Regulations are also in place to give employees a better work–life balance in defining work schedules, days off, and length of shifts. Peter is now paying for Paul's indiscriminate use of long work hours with double shifts; closing and then opening with insufficient time for rest; and inconsistent and split days off as a motivation to earn more income because of low wages.

Peter feels punished for the sins of Paul. He would argue that one size does not fit all. Each restaurant is unique in the segment and community it shares. He will further argue that tipping is so generous, employees generally wear broad smiles on their faces— which change to a stern stare-down when full disclosure of tips is required. Employees will offer up charge tips, as these are already known, and keep cash tips as a closely guarded secret. It's no different from operators who lament the inconvenience caused by the "system breakdown" and "can only take cash at this time" for a day part or a meal period.

Keeping the status quo works best for this group, and operators find restaurant-specific ways to even the disparity of wages earned between the front-of-the-house staff and the back-of-the-house and support staff. We will refer to this as group A. In this model, tip employees tell the employer when tips and wages in aggregate fall below the federal minimum-wage law.

Group B in this segment are those operators who pool all tips. Tip earnings of all service employees are intermingled and then redistributed. This must be totally voluntary and initiated by the employees themselves, with or without the knowledge of management, and not made part of the terms of hire or conditions of continuing employment. This means that an employer may not be involved in a tip pool beyond the administrative function of distributing tips charged on credit cards according to a formula devised solely by the affected employees.

The DOL has given owners some wiggle room. If employees have decided to pool tips and further agreed that the employer should play a part in the collection and/or distribution of the pooled tips, it is reasonable for the owner to demand that the terms of the tip-pool agreement be put in writing. The employees should put the terms of the pool in writing and give it to the owner with a list of participating employees. If the employees refuse to put it in writing, the employer could refuse to participate in the collection/distribution. This is an essential defense for employers and should be implemented where tip pools are in place. An employer is also permitted under New York law to consider the gratuity pool funds as employee property and discipline an employee for misappropriating or stealing such funds, just as an employer would presumably discipline an employee for stealing another employee's personal property.

Two legal cases set the precedent in Portland, Oregon, for employees to keep their tips on one hand or pool tips to be shared by nontip employees on the other. I am sure these cases were noted elsewhere to complete the groundwork for picking a side on this debate to arrive at a unified and structured wage scale where every employee feels valued and compensated fairly and operators get a fair return on their investment. To do so, operators must share with customers their plan to uplift employees while continuing to provide excellent service and quality food. You may be surprised how understanding your customers and employees really are.

Tipping is more prevalent in food-service operations than in any other service industry where employees depend on tips to supplement their wages. It still is subject to customer discretion more than any suggested amount. Now tip jars can be found near every point-of-sale terminal, from the smallest neighborhood joint that offers to-go food service to the big wine bucket at your favorite bar.

How much to tip is further divided by the segments of the industry. From the neighborhood deli and fast food to the cities' casual and fine-dining establishments to theme family concepts in the suburbs to the sea and sand locations to private clubs with golf, spa, and tennis amenities and casinos ... all tipping is discretionary based on one's own experience and the occasion on which you choose to dine out or use the amenities provided. Even at special occasions and catered events like weddings, where a gratuity is often included in the price to the host, guests attending the event still tip the service workers based on their experience and engagement with the service staff, from the parking valet to the bathroom attendant. No amount of persuasion, by whatever means, can make a customer tip a service worker if he or she had a poor experience.

Yes, indeed, tipping expectations have changed. Everyone expects it. What is not said or known is the fact that service workers are not paid fairly, and they depend on tips to supplement their wages. They often find creative ways to make up the difference from their employer. The operators know this, and know that they cannot police employees 24/7. So they have a built-in bias toward this expectation and manage employees from that perspective.

The operating cost of a food-service establishment is creeping up, and to keep abreast of changing customer behavior, food trends, and technology, operators are adding amenities to customer service and benefits to employees to keep them both happy and loyal. It's little surprise to find operators taking every opportunity to add a mandatory gratuity to the bill, from 15 percent to 25 percent on average based on the size of the party, so that living and fair wages can be obtained for employees through a tip pool.

The adversity of the changes in consumer behavior creates a mishap when operators add more employees to touch-points in the customer-service experience to lessen the waiting time for ordering in any restaurant segment at the front of the house, corresponding to increased ticket orders at the various kitchen stations, compounded by the need for fresh, made-to-order cooking that is the desire of customers today. Labor costs and profit margins become unsustainable when increased employee productivity and technology are not in sync. Ingredient alignment, menu choices, service style delivery, and technology are the clear choices for the future.

Customer service is a team sport. Whether to tip or not, and how much, is an individual decision of each guest based on that individual's own set of expectations for the food, beverage, and service experience performed by the team to be shared by the team.

Those who make a living balancing trays on their hands while maneuvering though tight space in a dining room, pouring beverages into boutique glasses, using knives with the skill of a brain surgeon to cut fruit, vegetables, fowl, fish and beef and creating artistic expressions with flour, eggs, butter and sugar you are the public face of the Food Service Industry.

Strategically, your work can be a source of differentiation and often the deciding factor that distinguishes one restaurant from the other. Management has strong roles to play in creating a climate in which good service, creativity, innovation and development of the service worker is the norm.

Operators who establish policies and procedures that emphasize style of service performance are service enthusiasts, those who stress maintenance of systems and processes are service bureaucrats. This results in a gap between the employees' own service orientation and that of management, to say it differently, the Food server has to hide his or her true feeling of wanting to satisfied a service request from the customer and present the face of management to follow procedures that say" we are sorry we are not allowed to do that" this ambiguity, and conflict, followed by feelings of dissatisfaction and frustration on the part of the employees leads to low morale and employee turnover not to mention stress and dissatisfaction.

When procedures are used to create climate for service an environment can result in which employees are encouraged and supported to give good service. Research has shown that when employees think that there is a strong service orientation and that they being supported in their desire to give good service, then customers are offered a higher standard of service and reflect backs a corresponding increase in satisfaction, retention and loyalty.

Being part of the community is another role of the Food Service worker that is often underutilized. . It is the links the restaurant has with the neighborhood within which it operates. The Manager connects with other community leaders to volunteer and or sponsor a community event with Food and Service that your employees are passionate about. .The goodwill created reflects and illuminates your restaurant in the community as a responsible and caring citizen.

The Chef, Butcher, Food Server, Bartender and Pastry Artist are consummate professionals and work under stressful, fast pace environment. Where else can you take raw materials, fresh vegetables and starches, herbs and spices, meat, fowl or fish and complete the manufacturing process wash, clean, slice, chop, dice, sauté,broil, grill, bake, mix, reduce, assembly, garnish and deliver to the customer waiting to consume it at the Dining Room table or Bar Stool. There is no shelf life, no test drive option, just instant gratification or deflated expectation.

Here are some attributes that were used to recruit Food Service workers by an employers who advertised recently on a popular website. I have made a notation on the side to suggest the ideal candidates. The roles service workers play to provide customer satisfaction is complex and uniquely theirs. With all the glamour, diverse ethnicity, personalities and cultural traits to blend into a high performing team is an opportunity to create a special service style to match your food and décor for a "wow" customer experience.

- *LOOKING FOR FUN PEOPLE TO JOIN OUR TEAM.* –*Dancing with the stars*
- Must have a personal vision of service and hospitality- Managers
- Guest focused & guest driven individuals- Personal Trainer
- Team players- LeBron James
- A positive dining experience through excellent product knowledge –Salesman
- Neat and clean appearance a must-. Model
- Be quick on your feet-. Usain Bolt
- Engaging and enthusiastic but not to chatty -Psychologist.
- Have superb communication skills- Lawyer
- Have a cheerful and outgoing personality- Bank teller
- Have a sincere desire to serve guests – Priest
- Organized and can multi-task without breaking a sweat – Accountant
- Can walk and stand for a long period of time - Police Officer.

Does this person exist? No wonder there is such a high turnover rate. Solution - select carefully, orient properly, train continuously and reward generously and develop internally.

The next time you dine out at a full service restaurant tip generously and get an autograph you just might have being served by the next big star of screen, stage, politics, medicine or sports.

Chapter 2

EMPLOYEE POINT OF VIEW

For customers to buy into this change of practice to no tipping, employers have to sell the story of their employees' commitment, dedication, professionalism, urgency, and delight to serve and fulfill every service request when customers choose to dine. Customers must understand that food-service workers' desire to serve is only restrained by the operator's discretion to balance customer satisfaction with prudent operation policies. To put it differently, do not be upset with your server when a service request goes unfulfilled or extremely grateful when the server takes personal responsibility to surpass guidelines to meet your needs graciously with a broad smile.

Food-service employees work every weekend and holiday at the expense of their own family and friends to serve yours because they love the business, the teamwork, and the camaraderie of creating an experience collectively every day for the enjoyment of you, the customer. Servers' days are long, and they don't end until the last customer leaves satisfied with a desire to return. These employees put team before self.

The employees' perspective on tipping, wages, and benefits was brought to the forefront in a recent study on the impact on pay fairness of a comparison between the compensation of hourly pay workers in the rank and file and that of their leaders in the corporate suites. Findings by Glassdoor chief economist Andrew Chamberlain suggest that a wide gap between hourly workers and their leaders can have a diminishing effect on morale. This was based on an analysis of over 1 million CEO approval ratings from current and former employees.

Further probing on this issue—supported by my own experience—found that gender, age, and education did not influence the view of a general manager or other higher executives when their pathway began. The CEOs with the highest ratings were the founders of the company followed by internally promoted CEOs. How I felt from my experience is, "If they can do it, so can I." That is a powerful incentive and tells a story of the culture of the organization. When workers are happy with their leadership and their prospects for advancement, that has a halo effect on how they perceive the CEO.

You do not see all employees, but they are there mixing your favorite cocktails at the bar in signature boutique glasses and thinking up new creative drinks for your next visit. Others are up in the wee hours in the morning waiting for trains and buses, in a hurry to create expressions with fruits, flour, sugar, butter, and eggs for your enjoyment. Still others enjoy the rush of adrenalin that athletes get when the whistle or bell is sounded to begin balancing trays in one hand while maneuvering between tables in tight spaces to get your food and beverage order to you just in time.

And when all is said and done, the cleanup crew works diligently to reset the kitchen and dining room to appear clean, like the operating room of a hospital ready for the next surgery, or in our case, the next meal period. They smile at every dirty dish, pot, and glass delivered to their stations like doctors and nurses do to their patients getting ready for heart surgery. Kitchen assistants are courteous to the food server carrying trays with food, giving them the right of way when transporting supplies from storeroom to kitchen, because they know the priority.

The butcher uses knives like a brain surgeon removing a tumor without damaging nerve endings when carving out the skirt steak from the diaphragm of the cow. The chef creates flavors and textures with ingredients to delight your tongue. The utility person takes ownership of sorting the recyclables because he cares about protecting the environment.

The maintenance crew keeps the physical plant—electrical and mechanical systems—in top shape for your comfort and enjoyment year round. Some employees are bridge-crossers using their on-call or part-time status to attend to their other life of rehearsals, auditions, readings, writing, painting, sculpting, or attending classes to transition to a future of fun, passion, and self-actualization. They never truly love our business the way some of us do who find purpose and joy in serving others. It fits nicely into their lifestyle while crossing the bridge to their future "real job"—like so many others before them who went on to fame and fortune while crediting their humble beginning in food service.

The passion demonstrated behind the scenes in preparation of ingredients and the setup of the dining room or event space for what is seen during service is a thing of beauty. The aggregate thousands of pieces of tableware handled and polished daily; the chopping, dicing, and slicing of ingredients; the crisp starch and pressed linen of tablecloths and napkins—all these make an incredible visual of teamwork at its best. This passion can be caught if you stay around it long enough for it to become a lifestyle. Therefore, seeking compensation commensurate with the output is deserving and justifiable.

On the other hand, some employees put self before team. They are so egocentric they prefer the status quo because it fits their characteristics perfectly. They engage in customer profiling, and once they identify a good tipper, that customer becomes "my customer." These employees will jump every hurdle to get their way for the customer service request. They will jump the line waiting for drinks at the bar or do it themselves. They will curry favor with the cooks to get their food order first. They are usually "too busy" to separate, scrape, and stack the tableware at the sanitation station for the dishwasher because it's "not my job." They fits into that group A category of restaurant employee mentioned earlier. Teamwork is not in these individuals' vocabulary.

When changes occur, these employees are the first to resist any disruption to their routine. Managers and owners love and hate then simultaneously, because customer feedback is so positive. They become untouchable because they appear to be passionate about this one table's dining experience on this day and time, to the detriment of all others. They compete ruthlessly for weekend dinner shifts when tips run high; ask to pick up additional shifts when bills are due or late; then becomes unavailable or are a no-show for Monday's lunch because of family emergencies. These "hurricane" workers are disruptors and can cause immense damage to an otherwise smooth-flowing team when they don't get their way. Eventually, mangers discover the internal storm gaining strength and must take action for the greater good of the team.

Anyone can do that for one table or two to make their tips. Those who excel will be willing to do it consistently for every table and every guest, regardless of the size of the tip, because they know the customer will return again and again to keep the team employed and more than likely leave a bigger tip the next time around. They work within the boundary of standards established for the team to succeed and not at the expense of supporting team members.

Maintaining a stable emotional state is a key attribute to overcome the reactions to being stiffed and to overly generous tippers. A week with a spate of cheap diners should not affect workers' ability to survive. Therefore, supporting the increase in the minimum wage and removing the tip credit from employers will go a very long way to bring into balance the uncertainty of wages and tips in the food-service business. When the burden is shared by all stakeholders because each has "skin in the game," together they can withstand the bumpy ride whenever it occurs.

Service which is rendered without joy helps neither the servant nor the served. But all other pleasures and possessions pale into nothingness before service which is rendered in a spirit of joy.—Mahatma Gandhi

Chapter 3

OPERATOR'S POINT OF VIEW

There is no sure way to restaurant success. Owners' traits are as diverse as there are reasons to own. Perhaps it is better to be an objective observer with analytical skills rather than a passionate "people person" prepared to serve away your time and money in pleasing customers and employees while practicing your craft in the kitchen or dining room. In return, customers become so spoiled and employees so complacent that when changes have to occur in raising prices and speeding up work rates, it is the operator who appears to be the bad guy and has to wait for acceptance of the new norm or duck for cover and close. This reminds me of a Caribbean proverb: "While the grass is growing, the horse is starving."

We have arrived at an intersection of trend and technology where you have to take all the good attributes of past restaurant practices of "scratch cooking," where you made everything from scratch—sauces in the kitchen, bread and pastries in the bakery and pastry shop, and beef and poultry cuts from the butcher shop, all on site—and combine it with the present explosion of global cuisine; the availability of fresh and frozen ingredients to support it; and techniques like sous vide, a method that involves partially cooking food and then vacuum-sealing and chilling it; later, it is reheated in a water bath to a precise controlled temperature to deliver super-juicy flavor-packed results every time.

An overabundance of restaurants without an uptick in dine-out occasions; soaring rents; escalating wages; and increased government regulation combine to cause anxiety and shake an owner's sustainability. Owners wonder whether customers will rearrange their budget by reducing their cable bill, their service plan for mobile devices, and other expenses to afford higher prices restaurants must charge to offset the higher cost of operation and still meet customers' lifestyle trends and technology usage in a want-it-now world.

This is why it's better to be an objective observer with analytical skills and forgo your love for doing things yourself in favor of purchasing from others, so your selling price is in sync with your production cost, with a sufficient amount left over to justify your time. To operators who are sitting on the fence to see what is happening within your competitive set, city, and state, this narrative is for you. This group reminds me of those who go to the gym and hold a pair of twenty-pound free weights, hoping that just by lifting these, they will suddenly gain sculptured biceps. You can use your own body weight to exercise and get the same result. Start with your own restaurant, trimming fat and waste to gain muscle and endurance to go the distance of change and win.

The loss of key employees is an operator's worst nightmare. Great employees are always willing to bet on themselves and take their chances with a "tip house" rather than work for a flat higher pay rate. This fear is compounded by the snowballing of concept and cuisine restaurants and a shortage of competent staff to support this expansion. They are risk-takers who like the uncertainty, randomness, and unpredictability of the business and who may be seated in their station today. Well-publicized stories on television, social media, and other mediums show diners randomly leaving extraordinary large tips for employees, just from overhearing a conversation regarding the struggle employees face making ends meet. Sometimes it's celebrities, athletes, or entertainers leaving those tips, not your average Joe or wannabe seeking publicity. Either way, there is an expectation of a great outcome from your service persona, engagement, and attentiveness to fill every service request.

Owners also fear losing customers and market share as they

raise menu prices to pay higher wages. It is never easy being an early adopter of a new operation model. You will lose customers anyway, because if you do not plan and prepare for changes—be it in customer behavior, food trends, or as in this case, regulatory legislation—you are planning to fail. You might as well start doing due diligence with your customers, employees, suppliers, and other stakeholders on what impact the legislation will have on your operation.

Begin visualizing what the new model of operation will look like and start planning. Even though you may keep the status quo after doing your research, at least you have a plan in place as changes continue to occur. You are better prepared for the future than those without a plan. Unless a catastrophic failure occurred previously and the lessons learned cemented the importance of planning, they are quite content to wait it out. "This too will pass," I have heard operators say. Others boast of how well their other restaurants are doing in Florida and are prepared to move there, where restrictive legislation does not exist.

There's also fear of the landlord to contend with. Lease negotiations can destroy a restaurant when combined with increased wages, according Andrew Rigie, executive director of the NYC Hospitality Alliance, a trade association that advocates and represents its members in hospitality, including restaurants, hotels, and clubs. The organization constantly hears from members about the financial burdens posed by escalating rents in New York City. The most common complaint was shorter leases and increases in rent, which make it impossible to remain profitable. Once the arithmetic comes out negative, owners do the honorable thing and say goodbye to the space, customers, and employees they have come to love like their next to kin.

Increases in wages, regulation, and law enforcement have created another layer of anxiety. In response, the National Restaurant Association has launched the Restaurant Law Center, a new organization that will advocate for restaurant owners and customers through the courts. The center will provide protection and advancement for the industry, including fighting against the government's regulatory overreach on a local, state, and federal level. How many restaurants may have to close before the impact is felt? Again, the Caribbean proverb "while the grass is growing, the horse is starving" applies. Operators' bank accounts will shrink significantly.

The regulatory environment has changed and will continue to change as municipal governments create legislation for the new economy. A myopic view of current issues affecting a segment of business or community results in legislation similar to poorly baked bread that fails to rise to the wholesomeness required to serve a general population. It meets opposition equal to the corrected quality and quantity of ingredients that should have been used in the first place.

Adjustments result in so much time extension, public hearing, and rewriting that those operators who were never going to purchase the new bread have time to squeeze all the profits out of customers and employees—and some cases landlords—and close shop suddenly without notice. To those operators, whose mind-set mirrors the old Garland ovens and stoves used to bake and cook, I say that they have done an extraordinary service to our industry by leaving. I invite a wide cross-section of the food-service community to provide comments, suggestions, and new ideas to mitigate one-size-fits-all legislation that disregards the many moving parts by segment and location that food service has.

Now we are left with operators who value their employees and customers enough to offer paid sick leave, vacation and personal days, profit-sharing, and pension plans. Customers can enjoy a wide variety of fresh, healthy, organic dishes to fit their health and fitness lifestyle, rather than genetically modified, high-fructose, processed, heart-clogging, mood-altering foods for a quick addicting buck. Customer loyalty will only increase.

Enterprising operators know that, with continuous training of the team to learn more about food and wine, recycling, cost of tableware, and the skills of great service and hospitality, employees will feel more confident about their role and perform more efficiently. They also know that every individual task in restaurant operation is directly related to all others and creates a cause-and-effect scenario at both ends of the service chain. Performing every task to completion by the standards established will ensure both employee and customer satisfaction. Is this the only way to survive extinction?

Chapter 4

Customer Point of View

Tipping is a function of one's propensity to spend on special occasions, which is not always in sync with one's ability to earn. To ask customers to join the debate on whether to tip or not and how much is akin to going to the doctor and saying, after your visit and treatment, "Depending on how you make me feel, I will add something extra to your fees."

Doctors take an oath to treat the sick to the best of their ability, preserve patient privacy, and teach the secrets of medicine to the next generation. A similar principle must be applied to hospitality. Serve each customer with courtesy, kindness, and congeniality. Pass on the secrets of hospitality to the next generations. Preserve the privacy of customers when necessary, as social media today can contradict privacy privileges.

When customers' calculation of tip percentage is removed from bills and becomes "hospitality included," then tip profiling cannot occur—as this can lead to customer profiling and a lower service level to match your tip profile. Customer confusion occurs when a service charge is added to a bill for a party of six or more, as some restaurants do. Perhaps someone in the party leaves additional tips, not knowing tips were included. In such a case, you never hear the server explain that the tip was included.

On a recent vacation trip to Miami, we stayed at a high-end national-brand hotel. We booked two rooms because we had extended family traveling with us. As we were taken to the rooms by the bellhop, we went first to our room. I tipped him for bringing the bags up for both rooms. When he went to the next room, he was tipped again. This time he was given a $100 bill by a close relative who mistook it for a $1 bill.

When I learned of the incident, I reported it to the front office manager. The next day, I waited for the employee to report for work. He had changed his hairstyle and wore shades to conceal his identity. To make a long story short, although I appealed to his moral conscience that an eighty-six-year-old guest would not tip you $100—in this case, $101, because she thought it was two $1 bills—nothing was ever done.

Chapter 5

LAWS, REGULATIONS, AND COMPLIANCE

To bring into balance the overwhelming advantages policy makers, regulatory agencies, advisory boards, and the commissions of enquiries continue to have, the food-service industry is beginning to create layers of practical, experienced leaders to form innovative groups to saturate all levels of government and get seats at the table in matters affecting food service, from design to delivery. The Restaurant Law Center, an arm of the National Restaurant Association, is one such effort.

The Restaurant Law Center is expected to file a petition for writ of certiorari or cert petition as its first order of business on behalf of the National Restaurant Association, asking the court to take up Oregon Restaurant and Lodging, et al v. Thomas Perez, et al. This case challenges whether the Department of Labor (DOL) has the right to enforce tip-credit restrictions on employers who pay employees the full minimum wage or more and who do not take tip credit towards minimum wage obligations on the distribution of tips. This petition seeks to unravel DOL's unfair interpretation of tip-pooling rules, following a split ruling by the Ninth Circuit Court of Appeals.

Finding ways to include all employees in the sharing of tips by pooling tips is illegal. However, the benefits trump the status quo. Keeping the status quo—and thus allowing the service worker who is in direct contact with customers to keep all tips and earn three to four times more than other team members—is demoralizing. This can lead to a decline in good customer service, as service workers can engage in customer profiling and focus only on those customers they believe will give a bigger tip. Customer satisfaction will deteriorate, as not all customers will be treated equally, and employers' profit will decrease.

That's why the first thing the Restaurant Law Center will do is ask the US Supreme Court to hear the case brought by several state restaurant associations on behalf of restaurants fighting the Department of Labor's anti-tip-pooling stance that prevents cooks and dishwashers from receiving tips. When the case is vetted by the Supreme Court and a ruling is made, it will cause further disruption for the food-service industry. When operators pay above minimum wage and do not take a tip credit and then share "pool tips" with everyone as they do in Nevada, the cooks and sanitation team members win.

When employers take a tip credit, they pay below the minimum wage and are required by law to make up the difference when tips plus the wages do not meet the federal minimum wage scale. When it is more, food servers are fighting to keep all their pool tips and share only with bussers or similar employees, as they do in New York. It's reasonable to believe New York is preparing for the worst-case opinion of the court, as Governor Andrew Cuomo recently announced that he will hold public hearings to examine whether he should eliminate the tip credit. Either way, nontipped employees are moving closer to a better standard of living.

It was interesting reading and learning how cases have been constructed over the history of the topic to arrive at the present opinion and order of the court. Ambiguous sentences are scrubbed for clarity, and each side argues for its version of intent, with the court having the final say. When laws are passed to protect one class that is specified, does it mean other like classes are open for regulatory overkill by extending and expanding control over the same law to the class that was unspecified or similar classes?

I strongly suggested and highly recommend that you read the

complete arguments, orders, and opinions of the two cases: Cumbie v. Woody Woo Inc, February 23, 2010, and the Oregon Restaurant and Lodging Association v. Perez, September 6, 2016, US Court of Appeals for the Ninth Circuit Court. The cases are super-critical to the food-service industry in understanding how we arrived at this juncture and the implications the opinion of the court will have on the operation, effectiveness, and sustainability of restaurants.

The DOL is concerned that "if there are no restrictions on an employer's use of its employees' tips when it does not utilize a tip credit, the employer can mandate that employees turn over all of their tips and use those tips to pay the minimum wage or for any other purpose." Although this is technically true, one suspects that most employers would find such business practices unwise.

But the beat goes on, with the drums getting louder across the nation for employees to be paid a living wage. It reminds me of a professor from Austria visiting at the University of Nevada, Las Vegas, to teach an economics class. This professor said that when business doesn't do the right thing, it allows government policy makers to correct and fill in the gap. It is quite obvious for all to see the insane profits and compensation paid to executives in the fast-food segments for decades without a thought for the frontline employees who drive those profits.

The challenge with government intervention in business operations, as is the case in food service, is that one size does not fit all, just as one medicine cannot cure all sickness. Policy-makers do not have a good understanding of the many intricacies of our business and need guidance and input from operators and advocacy groups who represent our industry. It's the independent operators who get squeezed.

The New York Hospitality Alliance, advocating on behalf of its members at all levels of government, supports pro-growth public policy, encourages investment in and promotion of NYC's hospitality industry, and evaluates the development, implementation, and fairness of relevant government regulations. Andrew Rigie, the executive director, is fond of saying he got his apron dirty by working in multiple positions within the industry before becoming an advocate. He is a rising strategic leader with a vision and mission to shorten the arms of government overreach for the food-service industry.

Another group formed to assure owners and operators that past legislation will not penalize future opportunities, formed within the Department of Small Business Services of New York City government, is the NYC Food and Beverage Hospitality Council. It is an alliance of more than thirty leading NYC industry professionals and businesses dedicated to promoting the sustained growth of the local food and beverage industry.

As operators prepare for the higher minimum wage, personal time off, sick days, and other benefit requirements yet to be written and implemented by government regulators, they have to rebalance their operating model to achieve greater efficiencies to offset this increase in labor cost. There is a consensus among some to eliminate tipping altogether in the high-end full-service segment. In the casual middle segment, with the national chains and independents, adding a predetermined service charge is gaining strength as a solution. The fast-food segment may turn to robotics and more technology. In all segments, owners and operators will turn to a combination of technology and increased training to incorporate a service-team approach to enhance the customer experience. Still others will move to states like Florida where the cost of doing business is more favorable.

Whichever path restaurateurs take, labor costs are on the rise. What started as a Fight for Fifteen in the fast-food segment has impacted, disrupted, and had unintended consequences in the safe haven of high-end full-service restaurants, which can cushion the blow to survive, and the marginally fragile middle segment and independents, which this shock may tip over a deep precipice of oblivion.

It is not only increasing wages that is keeping restaurant owners up at night but the nightmarish workload associated with keeping track of all the laws, rules, and policies to stay in compliance. Violations have created a whole new body of work for the legal profession, and more government workers have been hired to enforce the new laws and regulations. Now, lawyers are actively chasing disgruntled employees who were stiffed by employers for overtime pay, spread of hours, improper tip-sharing, and discriminatory hiring and promoting practices. It has become like an automobile accident where lawyers are partnering with other stakeholders to shake down insurance companies for injury compensation in the six figures.

Simply comply with all regulatory practices from the various federal, state, and local governments to avoid the sting of penalties, fines, and judgments from plaintiff's lawyers. In New York, Governor Cuomo had launched a new Enforcement and Outreach unit to ensure that workers are being paid what they earn. Employers who disobey the law will be held accountable.

Chapter 6

OCCUPATIONAL SAFETY AND HEALTH ADMINISTRATION

A nother folder in the restaurant owner's inbox to be taken seriously is how to avoid increased inspection and fines from the Occupational Safety and Health Administration (OSHA) for unsafe working conditions. "An ounce of prevention is worth a pound of cure" is a safety phrase that is often repeated to bring awareness in workplaces to reduce preventable accidents such as slips and falls, burns, cuts, and lacerations. It can help reduce the cost of insurance, protect your business from expensive lawsuits, and keep employees safe now and in the long term.

There were more than 3 million reported workplace injuries in 2014, according to the Bureau of Labor Statistics, and a staggering 75 percent of those injuries occurred in service industries like restaurants, bars, and coffee shops. In August 2016, OSHA stiffened compliance requirements and raised its fines for the first time in twenty-six years. Businesses that commit willful and/or repeated violations face a maximum $124,709 penalty, up from $70,000. Lesser offenses and one-time infractions now carry a maximum fine of $12,471, up from $7,000, for each day the business remains out of compliance. OSHA plans to adjust these fines yearly to account for inflation.

OSHA inspections typically happen without advance notice and follow an employee complaint, a referral from a government agency, or a prior inspection. Here are four common industry risks restaurant owners can proactively address to make their workplaces safer.

1. *Hazardous materials.* Hazard communication (HazCom) requirements introduced by OSHA in 2012 should not be a surprise. But in June 2016, new materials were added to the list, including several common kitchen chemicals that many restaurateurs may not think of, such as degreasers, oven cleaners, and ammonia. The updated rules require restaurants to label the chemicals clearly and review specific materials-handling safety procedures with all workers. To prevent injuries from inhalation or skin exposure, make sure all employees handling these materials wear proper protective gear, including face masks and protective gloves.

2. *Slips, trips, and falls.* Slips, trips, and falls are the number-one cause of workplace injuries, according to OSHA. In a busy commercial kitchen, grease may build up near cooking stations and water may pool in high-traffic spots near dishwashers, sinks, and walk-in coolers. Keep a mop and bucket in an easily accessible area, and make sure spills and standing water are cleaned up immediately. Place antiskid mats next to the sink, dishwasher, and cooler—and in the kitchen's entrance—to deal with busy foot traffic from the dining area to back-of-the-house spaces.

3. *Cuts and lacerations.* Using knives, meat slicers, and other sharp tools can increase the risk of cuts and lacerations. Make sure all employees understand how to properly handle and clean slicing equipment and use knives safely. Keep a first-aid kit handy and regularly replenish bandage supplies as needed.

4. *Burns.* Regular interactions with hot ovens, boiling water, and deep fryers increase the likelihood that kitchen workers can get severely burned. Make sure everyone wears gloves,

aprons, hats, and proper shoes around hot equipment and tools. If a burn occurs, rinse the affected area under cool running water, bandage loosely, and seek appropriate medical attention. Some workers' compensation carriers offer hotlines where businesses can report or seek medical guidance for new injuries or illnesses. If your carrier offers such a resource, make sure managers know the number to call.

Any one of these hazards can result in a serious or even fatal employee injury or illness and trigger an OSHA inspection. Any workplace injury—even the most minor—should be recorded and documented in detail, including the date of the incident, the name of the injured worker, the accident details, and witness accounts. In case of a workers' compensation claim or OSHA inspection, proper record-keeping helps you cover your bases and stay in compliance.

Chapter 7

FOOD SAFETY

Everywhere food is served, food-service operators are legally bound to ensure that all food for human consumption is handled in a safe manner. The most efficient way is to carefully follow the ingredients from farm, pasture, and ocean to the customer's table. Monitor each step in the production, handling, and transportation of the fruits, vegetables, meats, poultry, and fish to your receiving area for time and temperature and decide whether there is any potential for the food to be made unsafe by any physical, chemical, and/or biological hazards before it gets to the cutting boards, chef's knives, ovens, and pots. The traditional old-fashioned way of checking doneness of meats with fingers and sight is no longer applicable today, as only a bimetallic thermometer or something similar will do.

According to the Centers for Disease Control (CDC), improper cooling of food is one of the major causes of food-borne illness. During improper cooling, food is exposed to the danger zone of 41°F to 140°F for much too long. This dangerous practice allows disease-causing bacteria such as *Clostridium perfringens* to multiply rapidly. This bacterium produces a toxin that causes diarrhea, fever, and abdominal cramps. Symptoms of the disease may appear eight to twenty hours after eating such food.

The CDC estimates that as many as 250,000 individuals are affected by *Clostridium perfringens* each year. Remember, improperly cooled foods still taste good despite being filled with dangerous disease-causing bacteria. The risk is very high in deep pots of soup or chili, sauces, gravies, stews, rice, chili, whole turkeys, and large

31

cuts of meat. These large volumes of food are difficult to cool down quickly. Further, these foods will be served to many individuals and therefore have the potential to cause great harm.

The NYC health code requires that all potentially hazardous foods prepared for later service, including leftovers, be cooled rapidly. This means that in the first two hours of cooling, the foods must be cooled from 140°F to 70°F or less, and then go from 70°F to 41°F within an additional four hours. To cool foods safely and minimize risk to customers, food temperatures must be taken and documented on a cooling chart, entering one temperature reading each hour.

Standard operating procedure for cooling each food item must be included on recipe cards. Food temperatures must be taken and documented on a cooling chart, entering at least one temperature reading each hour. Improper cooling is common because food workers vastly underestimate actual cooling times. Proper planning must be done in production to avoid preparing foods a day in advance of service and off-peak hours to avoid cooling and reheating operations. Before preparing foods like tuna salad, potato salad, egg salad, or chicken salad, the ingredients for these dishes should be chilled to 41°F. In this way the rapid cooling requirement will be avoided. Here is a list of five critical tips in food safety:

1. *Receiving.* Always use reputable suppliers. Check all food items upon receipt.

2. *Storage.* Implement FIFO (first in first out) to ensure stock rotation. Store at safe temperatures (41°F or below, except smoked fish, which should be at 38°F). Avoid cross-contamination by separating raw and cooked foods.

3. *Preparation.* Always use clean and sanitary equipment and utensils (preferably color-coded equipment). Ensure good personal hygiene. Always prepare foods in small batches. Always cook foods to a safe temperature (poultry, stuffed meats, meat stuffings, 165°F; ground meats, 158°F; pork, 155°F; all other foods such as eggs, fish, lamb, etc., 145°F).

4. *Cooling.* Always cool foods quickly to a safe temperature (reduce temperature from 140°F to 70°F within two hours and from 70°F to 41°F within four additional hours or less).

5. *Reheating.* Reheat foods to a minimum temperature of 165°F within two hours. Monitor to ensure that control measures are working.

Chapter 8

FINANCIAL MODELS

Rising cost of ingredients, rent, utilities and yearly increase in minimum wages and benefits both from the Federal and State legislation across the country has intensified the pressure on Food Service Operators to seek new ways to operate in the most efficient and effective way possible to be sustainable. It calls for simplifying the operating process and procedures, elevating training and emphasizing teamwork, using technology and data analysis to meet and exceed the expectation of customers

As a sports enthusiast who always see the connection between a variety of sports performances with Food Service Management. In this case boxing, operators are repeatedly being hit with effective body blows over the course of fifteen rounds with their hands dropping, one more punch from any direction can be the knockout punch. The successful fighter train harder, collect data, studies his opponent tendencies to find the easiest way to win. There are literally hundreds of points in food service to counter punch the challenges operators face daily. We have provided a few critical ones as an example to compete.

Moving forward to create a new Operating model for long term sustainability requires new leadership. New Leadership that brings qualities that matches the changes necessary to succeed. Analytics and Technology will be the main drivers for success in the future. Combine with ethical leadership to lead from the front rather than the rear so the team does not scatter and get lost you make the "team feel love" a sense of ownership and connection supported by your underlying values articulated in, decision making and actions the more they are inclined to follow and respond in kind to the leadership direction for success.

Think about this for a minute. When employees wake up at 3 a.m. to catch the bus to the train and transfer to another bus to arrive on time for work, and they see the manager is already there gathering supplies and setting tables for an important early breakfast and later pouring coffee and clearing tables with them, how you think they feel? How likely are they to accept new direction and learn better ways to do old things? How likely are they to offer solutions to problems in their daily routine? How likely are they to feel relaxed and not tense up when the manager's around? How likely are they to want to be more productive and never be late or absent? You bet they will be motivated and pumped up.

This is one of the benefits you get with ethical leadership: twice as much effort out of employees. In the new model, this behavior can be quantified in more sales, more tips, and most importantly, more smiles. You cannot expect your team to perform with character and integrity if you don't set the example.

Writing alone cannot be effective and must be supported with analytics to be compelling and persuasive for operators who are fence-sitters and depend on instincts and emotions when facing the cold winds of change. I will create a profit-and-loss statement for an average healthy restaurant—with sixty seats open for lunch and dinner, and ten service employees working on average 150 hours a month—to show the before-and-after effects of the wages and benefits change on profitability when all else remains the same. I will then suggest strategies to offset the increase through training, technology, and menu improvement to sustain the same level of profitability. Lean in close as we begin.

Learning and Innovation

Here are some consideration should occupied your mind - how much more sales we have to achieve to cover this increase in labor cost to maintain the same level of profitability- is it likely, or alternatively how much savings we can achieve in other line items expenses to match the dollar amount increase in labor, and is it possible? Or can we use a combination of both increasing sales and reducing other cost to get back on track? How likely? You do not want to cut hours because it will hurt customer service which is paramount to where you are, and you are in a very competitive set.

Rational thinking is you must achieve some improvement in employee productivity. How much? And where? The simple answer is yes, get feedback from your employees ask them to offer suggestion, give incentives to get their best ideas. You will be surprise how much you will learn to streamline your operating system of processes and procedure in set up, service and reset while you set new targets for the team to achieve in sales. While researching application of technology best suited to your operation for further improvement in cost savings and sales enhancement. Looking forward you feels the dropping temperature from the cold winds of change, so you reset your thinking thermostat to apply an appropriate level of heat to remain in a comfortable profitable environment. It may mean using a team approach to raise the level of service, re-engineering your menu to streamlined your ingredients, and develop new creative, wholesome dishes for the team to upsell, cross sell and resell internally.

Externally constantly scanning the marketplace for change in the direction of the wind to make sure to the south your backend relationship with suppliers are reinforce to get great prices for fewer products in greater volume. To the north you have identified menu tablets to replace paper menus and eventually fewer servers as you begin a pilot program to determined its acceptance by the customer and how well it blends in to your operation work flow To the east and west you are searching for candidates to fill vacancies better suited with abilities and flexibilities to counter the wind of change from all directions.

After the deliberation it is time for a plan of action. You believed the best plan of attack is to use a combination of seeking cost saving in all line items expenses along with using the feedback from your team on ways to streamlining the operation of setup, service and reset the work flow process combined with training and incentive to arrive at a new sales target. Am a firm believer in constant improvement when feedback dictates or analysis discover emerging trends in likes of new amenities, cuisines or technology. New procedures for old processes gained from employee feedback. Keeping an open mind and being flexible in thought and deed is a critical factor in time of change.

Making adjustment to internal factors such as increase in wages, ingredients are controllable and variable. Developing solutions for a known outcome is easy. In this case increase in wages by $3,750.00. The first question you have to ask yourself can I increase by sales by X $ amount in Y many transactions to gain the contribution margin of Z to offset $3,750.00 increase in wages. Walk with me here.

Financial Objective and measures

To determine the sales amount you have to achieve to offset the $3,750 in wage increase. As an example, say your restaurant average check is $9.75 and your food cost for the ingredients on the plate on average is $2.80. Now you know your food cost is 28.7% and your contribution margin for every transaction is $6.95. You divide your wage increase of $3,750 / $6.95 contribution margin =540 as a rounded number. The result means you have to achieve 540 more transactions of $9.75 each for a total of $5,265.00 in sales to offset the wage increase every month of $3,750.00.

The formula is

- *Sale price – Cost of Sale = Contribution Margin / Increase Wages=# of transaction x Average check= Sales increase to cover wage increase*

Ingredients do not include paper products-napkins and bags, packaging-containers, plastic knife, spoon and fork or condiments. These items are best measured under separate categories. Now you ask yourself, is it possible?

To make it more manageable the amount of transactions can be further broken down to weekly, daily, and meal period or hourly transactions. As an example you are open six days a week, 14 hours a day and on average 26 days a month. This translates to an hourly rate when you divide the number of hours open in this example 26 days multiply by 14 hours equals 364 hours.

Next, you divide new total sales amount of $165,265.00 which includes the $5,265.00 to cover the cost of wage increase by the amount of hours open 364 equals to $ 4,540.25 in sales per month at the average check of $9.75.to meet the monthly increase in wages is 466 transaction per month.

The Formula is

- *# of days open for any period x # of hours open= Total Hours Open / New Total Sales Target = Sales per period / Average check=#of transaction per period*

You can calculate any other variable time period with this formula to arrive at amount of transaction targets. This formula can assist you to assess your financial picture at any time to determine whether to increase transaction as a result of falling average check or upselling to increase average check because of decrease in transactions.

Customer Impression

Now it may seem possible and can speak wisely from a financial perspective because you have a sales target to achieve and to motivate the team to the goal. So the next time a customer walks in your restaurant looks at the menu, ask a question, scans the ambiance, check out your personnel, smiles, and walk away is a miss opportunity to covert and enquiry to a sale. Similarly, when a customer make a special service request for replacing one ingredient for another because of dietary restriction on your signature dish which they desire to purchase the response quickly becomes "sure, will have the chef do it" instead of "Sorry, we cannot make changes to the dish" or "let me check with my manager" because everyone on the team is aware of the goal to increase sales and customer satisfaction because every transaction counts.. Additionally, when the host is seating customers faster than the service team ability to provide the level of service required then additional support staff is alerted to jump in to smoothen out the spike in activity. It similar to hospital emergency room where they use Code levels by color, name or numbers to indicate the degree of urgency needed for patients care. In other service segments when the amount of customers in line reach a certain numbers it triggers additional front line support to keep the line moving to avoid service delays. Training can be provided to make the team more sales friendly, engaging and confident to talk about your signature dish, special of the day or offer tasting to make a sale. In other words turn the first time visitor to a customer and loyal customers to advocates for your food and beverage. A good design and layout of your restaurant will allow a line of sight to keep an eye on customer movement in and out of the store. Loyal customers are good candidates for upselling and reselling food and beverages by the team. When sales alone is not sufficient you will know daily and can begin additional measures tomorrow rather than waiting for the mole to become a mountain at the end of the month.

Internal Solutions

Alternatively, you may consider using Menu Tablets instead of paper menu at the tables for ordering this may reduce the number of servers needed and reduce your labor cost. You may examine the usage of paper products, packaging and condiments and set standards in the amount to complement each order. Reducing the ratios for chemicals to water solution for cleaning will make a contribution. Or any combination of these initiatives to equal $3,750 increase labor cost. You can also compare and contrast your labor cost in dollars and hours worked versus the cost to serve one customer and the amount of time it takes to serve. Stay focus on the formula as an example.

The metric cost to serve a customer is:

- *Total Wages and Salaries / Total Customer count= Cost to serve one customer*

In our example it is $52,000 divided by 4395, equals $11.83 cents and is it justify for the service delivered. You may discover new insight in scheduling.

Another metric is time to serve one customer is:

Total customer served / Total hours work = Time to serve one customer

The formula is the amount of customers served 4395 without consideration for additional transaction with the wage increase, divided by the number of hours worked 1600 is equal to 2.74 hours. It was calculated this way intentionally to give you alternative practice in calculating the before and after effects of cost increase in whatever variable comes up in your operations as we did the "after the wage increase" in calculating the amount of transaction needed.

Again is it reasonable for set up, service and reset.

Now you can break it up into smaller pieces to get to the efficiency rating for servers to match each component of what they do, and how they spend their time doing it. Now you can ask questions on how and when is the best time to do it and even is it necessary or a better way? There are as many ways to improve efficiency as there are dishes on your menu.

Similarly, although rent is a fixed cost, you may look at this cost in many new ways to measure this independent fixed cost to the many dependent cost variables in your restaurant.

In the Profit and Loss Statement #1 where the rent starts $8, 000 per month as an example, you have 750 square feet of space. Let's dig into together and analyze how it speaks to its dependent family member's and how well it can be sustained and improve Sales, Customer Service and Employee's efficiency. In real estate parlance it cost $10.67 per square foot at $8,000 per month. In restaurant operation you have to match this metric with $213.33 in sales per square foot. Now you can speak intelligently of your business. With a known factor, it can be divided further into storage and preparation for employee's efficiency and service areas for customer service improvements and eventually to increasing sales.

As you continue to grow you can allocate more space to your service area and less to storage as you are get more frequent deliveries. The same is true when you decide to purchase pre-package fruits and vegetables and sous d vide cook proteins and soup products you will need less preparation space and equipment.

You measured the square footage used in each area. Subtract it from total available space to arrive at a more meaningful cost measurement. Measure storage and production area square footages separately from sales then using utility expenses spread evenly among all areas. Assign a portion of employees' wages and benefits to areas of storage, production and sales. As we continue smashing the numbers in smaller pieces.

You determined it to be 20-30-50 split among storage, production and Sales. When challenges arise you can now push or pull on the many measureable switches at your control to adjust to new operating norm. The point is the more ways you can view your operation the better you are able to make informed decision when challenges arise quickly

	Square Feet	Utility	Sales	Hours	Wages
Storage	150	800		160	10,400
Preparation	225	1200		640	15,600
Service	375	2000	160,000	800	26,000
Total	750	4,000	160,000	1600	52,000

An owner ask me once whether there is a specific size of space to allocate to storage and preparation versus service, a standard response is always one size never fit's all. First you start with what the legal requirements are in your jurisdiction if there is any. While there are industry averages for similar types you always have to fall back on your foundation pillars of what's your menu, how you going to serve it, where you are located and who your customers are. This information will tell you everything you need to have right down to the smile on your face when the numbers add up positively.

Sales			
Food	100,000	62.5%	
Beverage	60,000	37.5%	
Total Sales	160000	100%	
Cost of Sales			
Food	30,000	18.75%	
Beverage	12,000	7.5%	
Total Cost Sales	42,000	26.25%	26.25%

Gross Profit	118,000	73.75%	
Food	70,000	43.75%	
Beverage	48,000	30%	
Total Gross Profit	118,000	73.75%	
Controllable Expenses			
Salaries and Wages	52,000	32.5%	
Employee Benefits	8,000	5%	
Utility Services	4,000	2.5%	
Repairs and Maintenance	2,000	1.25%	
Marketing	250	.016%	
General and Administrative	4,000	2.5%	
Music and Entertainment	10,000	6.25%	
Legal and Accounting	600	.037%	
Total Controllable Expenses	80,850	50.53%	76.78%
Fixed Expenses			
Rent	8,000	5%	
Insurance	1,500	0.9%	
Depreciation	1,000	0.6	
Licenses and Permits	500	0.3%	
Loan Payments	3,000	1.8%	

Total Fixed Expenses	14,000	8.75%	85.58%		
Profit/Loss	23,150	14.42%	100%		
Income Taxes	4,630	2.89%			
Net Profit	18,520	**11.53%**		11.53%	✓

In P&L #1 above before wage increase shows earnings of $23,150 before Taxes looks good meaning you are slightly above the 10% industry average. In cost categories of Food, Beverage and Labor prime cost for restaurants is also within the norm. Food and Beverage cost of between 25-32% is normal but you should get nervous once it crosses the 30% mark unless of course you have some comparative advantages in the next two categories as an example a sweetheart of a lease deal on rent as is the case in our example or your style of service delivery can give you an edge in lower labor cost.

As the wage increase goes in effect there are multiple ways to measure the change in your restaurant. In the P&L #2 below indicate

Sales			
Food	100,000	62.5%	
Beverage	60,000	37.5%	
Total Sales	160000	100%	
Cost of Sales			
Food	30,000	18.75%	
Beverage	12,000	7.5%	
Total Cost Sales	42,000	26.25%	26.25%

Gross Profit	118,000	73.75%	
Food	70,000	43.75%	
Beverage	48,000	30%	
Total Gross Profit	118,000	73.75%	
Controllable Expenses			
Salaries and Wages	57,750	36.09.%	
Employee Benefits	8,000	5%	
Utility Services	4,000	2.5%	
Repairs and Maintenance	2,000	1.25%	
Marketing	250	.016%	
General and Administrative	4,000	2.5%	
Music and Entertainment	10,000	6.25%	
Legal and Accounting	600	.037%	
Total Controllable Expenses	86,600	54.12%	80.37%
Fixed Expenses			
Rent	8,000	5%	
Insurance	1,500	0.9%	
Depreciation	1,000	0.6	
Licenses and Permits	500	0.3%	
Loan Payments	3,000	1.8%	

Total Fixed Expenses	14,000	8.75%	89.12 %			
Profit/Loss	17,400	10.88%	100%			
Income Taxes	4,630	2.89%				
Net Profit	12,770	**7.98%**			7.98%	✓

Chapter 9

SOCIAL AND ECOMONIC TRANSFER

To tip or not is invariably tied to supplemented income for food-service industry workers because it is a well-known fact that dependency determines their social and economic class. The disparity of tips by segment can be immense, from the cocktail waitress at a high-end Las Vegas casino working with high-rollers in the baccarat pit on a winning streak to your neighborhood fast-food worker in the kitchen on a sweating streak. What started out as an effort to determine the minimum wage be for fast-food workers at McDonald's, Burger King, and Wendy's and make sure it's sufficient to provide a satisfactory living standard to reduce the level of public assistance has exploded to affect all segments.

Tipping has created internal strife between culinary and dining room employees. It produces two layers of pay, with deep social and economic consequences for each group. Tipping perpetuates an unfair and uneven pay system among and within each variable of gender, age, race, and task—and by extension, class. If this is allowed to continue, it becomes an issue of race, age, and gender discrimination and not teamwork with a focus on customer service. No one team member can give all customers the service experience they expect and deserve, making it so memorable that they can relax, feel at home, let go of their worries and stress, and enjoy extraordinary food and beverages. It takes a mix of personalities equal to the customers' mix to have such an impact.

This is where the saying "diversity is strength" comes into

play. Everyone receives the necessary training and orientation to maintain operating standards. Interaction with the customer, where all employees can release their uniqueness, is the secret sauce that completes the memorable experience.

Recently, a family member had surgery performed at a hospital rated best in class in the country, by a surgeon rated top-ten best in his specialty. Naturally, there is some level of comfort when you can secure the services of such a doctor to do his work at a highly regarded hospital. During the stay and follow-up care, we found the diversity of the staff in every area of operation matched our cultural uniqueness. Everyone from the head nurse on the floor to the attending RN to the food nutrition team taking the meal choices and delivering them—even to the doorman and valet parking guys—were all Caribbean persons. I do not know whether it was planned that way or a random coincidence of scheduling. It was a perfect example of how a service team's members can make you feel comfortable and relaxed and take away the anxiety of surgery.

Similarly, when you go out for a dining experience and you choose a highly rated restaurant with a celebrity chef, you know the food will be awesome. It is the service team's interaction with you that determines the outcome of the experience. So when I received a survey telephone call to respond to a question about the time spent at the hospital, I was delighted to share how special we felt. It was unexpected and an experience we will never forget. And of course, the family member is doing fine.

The government intervenes to bring into balance the opportunities the food-service industry creates for employment and concern for the value of the work performed, health, safety, and self-sufficiency. What is lost in the analysis is the quantity and quality of employees from other service professions like teachers, law enforcement, accountants, and bank employees who enjoy a second and third income from food service. It offers of flexibility, seasonality, income, a new circle of colleagues, and the instant gratification of serving the basic needs of life—food and drink—in a mirror and marble environment.

Okay, this may not apply to the fast-food segment. Still, the introductory lessons learned—like punctuality, accountability, and teamwork—are never lost and are transferable in the pursuit of future careers. In other words, it's a beginner's kit for the world of work.

The soft skill of getting to work on time is the hardest thing for teenagers, much less going to work at all when their friends are hanging out, whatever that means for today's teens in the era of social media. Where else can you learn accountability for every burger bun, patty, cup, and pack of condiments and dressing and now lettuce leaves? Each item may cost so little, but it rises to the level of a crime when you lose your job for giving one away to friends who visit your store—the same friends who frowned on you for going to work.

Putting on a uniform for the first time makes you feel weird and uncomfortable, even when it fits perfectly. You feel shame perhaps, and the outer limits of uncomfortable—until you get that first paycheck. Then your feelings begin to change. The uniform represents membership on a team with a single purpose of speed, accuracy, and service, with your smile and engaging attitude so the paychecks will continue and an increasing amount of money will flow into your bank account.

Oftentimes when we seek data to support and validate our thinking, it is not always primary to arrive at a conclusion. Extrapolation from a broader data set, observation, or secondary sources may be necessary. As an example, the New York State commissioner of labor at the time the wage board was convened to focus on the fast-food industry stated, and I quote, "My decision to convene the wage board was based on data and studies that indicate that 60 percent of fast-food workers in New York are in families enrolled in at least one public assistance program." Some of the studies found in the briefing document were based on the year 2014. Annual average employment in New York State size-of-establishment data for fast-food establishments found a total of 164,483 employees working in 15,418 establishments.

It can be argued that the amount of taxes paid by these establishments can be compared to the amount of assistance received by the families of these workers and see where it falls to accept the increase in the minimum wage or reject it because of the imbalance between paid taxes and government subsidies. In other words, government subsidies being greater than taxes received from their employers is an irrefutable reason to support wage increases, not any punch-in-the-gut feelings. To cry wolf about the loss of jobs and the use of robotics to replace "inefficient employees" making fifteen dollars an hour bagging fries as former executives cry—with an emphasis on "former" rather than "now"—is premature and discriminatory. The "now" CEO of McDonald's made an investment in employee wages and benefits and has already had a significant impact on customer service. Economists generally believe wage increases give money to the poor and leave less for the wealthy. On the other side of the pillow, economists have found that with a pay raise, poorer people will spend more of the extra income than the wealthy and therefore increase revenue in other areas of the economy and create more jobs.

The pregnancy of this debate must be carried to full term to see whether the winner will be robotics, technology, or the smiling, charming voice of a live person. In a diverse consumer population, there is a need for variable service delivery to match one's lifestyle with outlet types by location to meet dining expectations. Customers will have a choice of a fully automatic robotic experience at the drive-through window, and inside you will get an extremely limited service experience. Another option will be using a menu app from your favorite restaurant to order in advance so when you walk in or drive through, your food will be delivered to your table or window. At the drive-through, the cars will queue by order number.

Menu tablets at the table will replace order takers and food servers. There will only be food runners made up primarily of persons in white coats who had some part in the preparation of the dishes delivered to the table. Consumers will now have a menu of choices from an automatic robotic experience at one end of the service spectrum, where the human touch is not required, to the more polished and refined service delivery with style and grace, where you get a choice of sparkling or still water with your house-baked bread and house-cultured butter. Kelvin Alexander of Thrillist, an online magazine, put it bluntly: "What we're witnessing, as you see this rise of both the high and low end, is the hollowing out of the restaurant industry center—the gentrification of food, carried to its logical conclusion. You had something that was interesting and a great value, it attracted everyone, and now all that's left until a rebirth is extravagance or thrift." Well said, my friend.

In New York and across the nation, restaurant opening and closing continue, not only because of the soaring cost of rent, wages, benefits, and ingredients but also because of the shifting demographic population, in cities within states and neighborhoods within cities— especially the millennials, who want to be in cites and neighborhoods where it's "cool and hip." New immigrants from all corners of the world bring a heightened awareness of global cuisines, creating a perfect storm of geopolitical, economic, and social proportions. Meanwhile, technology is stretching to every facet of food service.

Operators who transition smoothly will give birth to a new era in food service in terms of when and how food is ordered, how it's served, where it's consumed, how it is merchandised, and where no tipping is allowed to bring the nation's roughly $782.7 billion restaurant business in line with modern workplace standards. Like every other disruption in our lives, it will take time to adjust to the new norm, but on reflection, we will be glad we did. After all, do you tip the nurse and doctor when you receive health care at the hospital?

This new era of food service will develop along the lines of other retail service providers like Ralph Luren, Polo, Nautica, and Nike, where the brand and branding are critical identifiers for success. Research and development time and space for new and innovative dishes from around the world have to be developed alongside regular kitchen operations from the diverse ethnicity of cooks and other team members. Customers want to enjoy the cuisines of the world without having to travel there.

The same can be said of improving the customer experience through sensory perception with the use of audio and lighting to go along with the size, shape, and color of the tableware. All this sensory stimulation before the food touches the tongue delights the brain. However, it's the small neighborhood food operators who can brand their experience with locally sourced ingredients, products, employees, and ambiance that are authentic to the community they serve.

Consumers want to know more and more about what they consume and what they feed their families. The specific information that is most sought may fluctuate from year to year, but there is no doubt that the thirst for information is here to stay. For some, this demand for transparency could merely be definitions of less-than-familiar ingredients or knowing what allergens might be present. For others, this could go as deep as understanding the company's values and positions on key issues of importance. Research suggests that companies that provide the broadest set of transparent information and allow consumers to explore as deeply as they'd like engender the most trust.

Brands are failing as the trusted source for what is in food products. In recent research conducted by Label Insight, nearly all respondents (94 percent) said that it's important to them that the brands they purchase products from are transparent about what is in the food and how it is made. Yet only 12 percent of consumers rank brands as their most trusted source for information about what is in their food. The largest food companies, in particular, are in trouble with consumers.

Chapter 10

THINKING FORWARD

The consumer's relationship with both food and the food industry will continue to change. Many more consumers will pay attention to the environmental impact of the food they buy and how sustainable it is. You see signs of this now with more plant-based diets and people eating lower on the food chain to reduce the carbon footprint of their consumption. Foods choices will not only evolve to reflect personal preferences for taste, convenience, and healthfulness but will also be a reflection of one's personal values—just as recycling is a behavior that signals one's care for the planet.

Transparency is certainly here to stay and is a prerequisite for trust between consumers and companies. The Center for Food Integrity found that 57 percent of consumers believe that big food companies put their own self-interest ahead of consumers', but that drops to 29 percent for small food companies.

Another sign of the evolving food scene is the uptick in food halls and pop-ups that are cheaper to run. They can be found in choice locations in neighborhoods all across the city as operators flee rent increases—although others, with deeper pockets to succeed where others failed, are literally gobbling up the spaces as they become available.

There are no reliable ways to capture how many restaurants have closed in the previous three years or for any period of time and determine the variables that caused the closures to build a compelling case that will move regulators to ease their overreach. Yes, higher rent and increased wages are definitely contributing factors; but what percentage do they contribute in relation to dependent variables such concept, food quality, ambiance, service, management, leadership style and qualities, and financial resources?

Until a definite structure is in place to quantify the independent and dependent variables, causes, and effects, mistrust will continue based on past practices. Advocates for restaurant owners are seeking to add an administrative fee to menus to offset the increasing cost of labor and wages. Regulators are asking for proof that any added fees will get to employees's pockets to even the disparity of wages between and among the various job categories. The argument from the regulator's perspective is that poor management and inappropriate timing, not high rent and labor costs, are the cause of increased restaurant closures, as the demand for new permits remains strong.

Subjective statements from restaurant owners are not sufficient to move the needle for regulators to act. Objective data is the bedrock of good policymaking, and studying important topics like restaurant closures using a methodology with arbitrary selection and capture characteristics—such as menu type, segment, service delivery, location, years in the industry, education level, number of employees and so many other variables—will ensure that the results accurately reflect the food service community. The time is now for advocates to partner with regulators to create a pathway with ease of access for all interested parties and begin a new level of trust that can be measured and transparent.

As operators have hidden behind federal minimum wages previously, now they want an administrative fee as a solution to escalating costs, with no assurance the administrative fee will flow directly to employees' wages. Then what happens when the Supreme Court rules in favor of restaurant associations to share tips with all employees? Will the administrative fee be repealed? A precedent for an administrative fee on menus will be difficult to turn back from, as is the case now with tipping.

Mobile app usage has taken off in the restaurant industry, and operators are eager to promote apps because they can drive use without adding point-of-sale terminals. Apps also let operators collect data more easily and may increase efficiency. The market for restaurant delivery is growing rapidly across the spectrum—from limited-service chains like Panera Bread to polished-casual concepts like The Cheesecake Factory to fast food giant McDonald's. Everyone wants a piece of it.

Consumers are demanding delivery to meet their more time-sensitive professional lifestyle. It is a niche market that will grow exponentially in the new economy, where consumers want everything now at the snap of their fingers simply because everything else is literally at their fingertips with smartphones. To restaurant operators, it's simply a new revenue stream without entry barriers to partner with technology courier companies for deliveries, such as UberEats, to get a sales lift that's incremental.

Have you noticed how many persons are eating while driving or sitting on buses and trains? Have you noticed that when you go to fill up your car at the gas station, you can also fill up your stomach? Have you noticed there is a prepared-food section at every grocery store? Have you noticed that when you go to the fishmonger to purchase fresh fish, you can also get some steamed or fried? You can get chips and dip along with your Tide and bleach at the laundry. There are "cool and hip" places to eat now at airports, arenas, and stadiums to bypass airline food and to watch your favorite team play.

Can you think of other human activities you can attach food too? It seems that adding a food and drink component makes everything better. We are social animals with an overwhelming need to connect. Before you open another restaurant, think about a connecting activity your customers like where food and drink play a supporting role. When the food and service are awesome, the experience is intensified to a lasting memorable event.

What piqued my interest on tipping were the cases in Portland, Oregon, and New York. They were complex—built up and layered over time by other opinions and orders on previous cases. The two cases from Oregon represent the most critical issue facing the food-service industry presently. Due to split opinions of lower courts, the issue has to ultimately be decided by the US Supreme Court. Hanging in the balance is whether cooks and dishwashers matter in the distribution of tips, on one hand, and whether employers can do whatever they please with tips on the other when a tip credit is not taken.

Tipping and wages are like Siamese twins joined at the heart and head in restaurants. The tipping amount determines overall wages earned, and by extension whether those wages can support independent living standards. The case earned a space in my mind because I earned extravagant tips as a student in Las Vegas working at the Golden Nugget Casino as an assistant restaurant manager. I was given a six-hundred-dollar casino chip one night as a tip, and I wasn't sure if it was a mistake or the customer was too drunk. I've also sweated profusely in kitchens earning minimum wage while exploring my creative side.

It is too soon to tell whether the no-tipping model will become a standard or simply an option for a few restaurants that can make it work. What is clear so far is that it has forced operators to take a hard look at their operation with a different outlook and make changes large and small for a new operating model.

The perfect storm of technology, increasing regulation, rent, and labor cost is applying increasing pressure to jettison the embedded practice of tipping and create a new pathway of higher flat wages. The greater good for all employees is served when there is no longer an expectation of a tip when service is provided. In today's new economy, at all other service providers—like your car mechanic, dentist, favorite retail stores—you never tip, unless it is a token for a known anniversary or event in the life of your service provider. Tipping is never required.

My interest in the tipping issue intensified when the Fight for Fifteen began. I became curious about the answer to the question: "What if restaurants were allowed to open only when the owner and/or operator pass a competency test in management skills of leadership, merchandising, customer service, financial acumen, sanitation, and cleanliness to reduce the failure rate?" It seems too many are opening restaurants because they can cook. They received a financial settlement, they wanted to have a business, they saw the other guy being successful, so they followed the "me too" syndrome.

There is a need for mom-and pop restaurants in small-town USA—as well as cozy, chic neighborhood eateries in major metropolitan cities—to gain access to financial and operational knowledge of systems and operating procedures. They must be able to match data and technology with customer behavior and food trends in service delivery, just the same as any of the national brands used for growth and development. I decided to build this bridge for sustainability to sharpen owners' focus on cost categories and act swiftly when significant changes occur. Make contingency plans to identify and prioritize risk; develop a plan to diminish the impact; and test the assumption of the new financial model.

Even then, rent hikes can cause the restaurant owner uncontrollable pain. The tricky part is figuring out how to survive when every other cost rises too. This book was designed to give owners and operators self-assurance and an example.

On Balance a closing argument in favor of eliminating tipping as we have seen a fair number of restaurants have closed citing mandatory wage increase along with other expenses. It's seems a perfect opportunity to leave because some of their practice of paying flat wages, shift pay, tips only, can no longer be hidden in the low end and independent segment to make up for incompetent management skill set while at the top end where tips flow exceedingly well it may have resonated mentally to share in the wealth "we created", "they are making so much" and add their non - service friends in the tip pool. In my work experience I had the pleasure of doing the payroll of the Banquet staff where they were making three times as much as I did. Only to think about how hard they are working every day and deserving of the rewards from the accumulated tips.

In no secret Food Service work is physical, repetitious, and time sensitive stressful in all segments the size of the space may change where you work as you move up the segment ladder what remains the same is close quarter of the production line cooks, high temperature in the kitchen, white male dominated culture with its own colorful kitchen language and jokes makes it challenging to absorbing different gender and races without feeling isolated or accepting the norm to fit in. Once you accept it as a norm you basically give up your human right to be respected as an individual and further deterioration and dehumanization as an object of their whim and fancy. A lesson to be learned the next time a steak is cooked in "their kitchen" observed the seasoning used in bringing out the flavor and deliciousness. It includes not only salt, but, pepper, a little parsley, finish with butter and garnish with a mushroom cap. The ingredients are not an option or an afterthought to get the best tasting steak. Most chefs value the recipes they know and the ingredients they use in creating their specialty dishes. Now is the time to transfer those values to those they work with. Change is difficult but necessary to think of and see all Food Service workers as equal it's a human right. Strength not only come from numbers but tied to purpose therefor sharing tip with everyone or eliminating it all together is where I draw the line.

BIBLIOGRAPHY

Alexander, Kevin. "Why the 'Hot New Food Town' Must Die." *Thrillist*, May 12, 2016. https://www.thrillist.com/eat/nation/why-the-hot-new-food-town-must-die.

Eisenpress, Cara. "Restaurants Are Seeing Their Profits Devoured by Landlords and Labor Costs." *Crain's New York Business.* http://www.crainsnewyork.com/article/20170123/HOSPITALITY_TOURISM/170129979/restaurants-are-feeding-their-lean-profits-to-higher-rents-and-growing-labor-costs.

"Food Service Operators." NYC Health. http://www1.nyc.gov/site/doh/business/food-operators.page.

Fox News. "NYT food critic Pete Wells calls tipping 'irrational, outdated, ineffective." September 4, 2013. http://www.foxnews.com/food-drink/2013/09/04/nyt-food-critic-pete-wells-calls-tipping-irrational-outdated-ineffective.html.

"Minimum Wage." New York State Department of Labor. https://www.labor.ny.gov/workerprotection/laborstandards/workprot/minwage.shtm.

"Oregon Restaurant and Lodging v. Solis." Leagle. http://www.leagle.com/decision/In%20FDCO%2020130610C45/OREGON%20RESTAURANT%20AND%20LODGING%20v.%20SOLIS.

Taylor, Kate. "McDonald's Ex-CEO Just Revealed a Terrifying Reality for Fast-Food Workers." *Business Insider*, May 25, 2016. http://www.businessinsider.com/mcdonalds-ex-ceo-takes-on-minimum-wage-2016-5?yptr=yahoo?r=UK&IR=T.

www.ingramcontent.com/pod-product-compliance
Lightning Source LLC
Chambersburg PA
CBHW021021180526
45163CB00005B/2059